AMERICA

THE LAND I LOVE

Previous Page: The corn fields of the Midwest seem to stretch for miles, such as in this scene of a farm near Ottawa, La Salle County, in North Central Illinois.

This Page: The *Natchez*, a stern-wheeler steamboat, still operates as a tour boat on two-hour trips around New Orleans Harbor.

AMERICA
THE LAND I LOVE

Thomas G. Aylesworth and Virginia L. Aylesworth

Bison Books

First Published in 1984 by
Bison Books Corp
17 Sherwood Place
Greenwich, CT 06830

ISBN 0 86124 143 6

Printed in Hong Kong

Acknowledgments
The authors and publisher would like to thank the following
people who have helped in the preparation of this book:
Abigail Sturges, who designed it; Barbara Paulding, who
edited it; John K Crowley, who did the photo research.

Picture Credits
All photographs courtesy The Free Lance Photographers
Guild, with the following exceptions: Virginia L Aylesworth,
88 (top) Florida Department of Commerce, 36 (top) Hawaii
Visitors Bureau, 94, 95 (right) J N Kettinger, 49 (below)
Diane Kirkland, 37 (top) Michigan Department of Commerce,
48, 49 (top) National Park Service, 36-37, 81 New York
Convention and Visitors Bureau, 20-21 Old Sturbridge
Village, 17 (top) South Dakota Division of Tourism, 47 (top)
State of Vermont, 16 Wyoming Travel Commission, 74-75

A farm in Pennsylvania near Lititz in Lancaster
County—the heart of the famous Pennsylvania
Dutch country.

Contents

Mount Shasta rises 14,162 feet above sea level in the Klamath National Forest in California.

Introduction

The United States of America — a beautiful land. The fourth largest country in the world both in size and population, America stretches the full width of the North American continent from the Atlantic to the Pacific, and also includes Alaska on the edge of the Arctic and Hawaii in the tropical Pacific.

From the warm beaches of Florida to the frozen Northlands of Alaska, from the Midwest prairies to the torrid deserts of the Southwest and the snow-capped mountains of the West, America is as varied as it is vast. America is the home of the spectacular Grand Canyon, the mighty Mississippi, the thundering Niagara Falls. Unbelievably rich in resources, this huge and beautiful country harbors some of the best farming areas on the globe in its vast stretches of fertile soil. Water is plentiful in most regions, and equally precious is America's great treasure trove of minerals such as coal, copper, iron, natural gas and oil.

Only about 300 years ago, most of what is now the United States was largely a wilderness. Europeans saw in this rich and spacious land an opportunity to build new and better lives, so they arrived, thousands upon thousands, from many countries. They brought with them a vast array of skills and ideas, contributing to America's colorful cultural heritage. And they brought the ideals of freedom and liberty, setting up a government designed to protect the liberty of all. They wrote a Constitution guaranteeing freedom of speech, freedom of religion, freedom of political belief and freedom of the press — a document like none other in the world. Out of diversity came unity.

The great size and wealth of the land has challenged every generation of Americans since the first colonists. Armed with freedom of thought and action, Americans embraced that challenge. When mountains blocked the way westward, roads and railroads were built around them, through them, or over them. When floods threatened farms and cities, dams and levees were built to hold back the water. Where rainfall was scanty, great irrigation systems were built to help grow crops.

America is still changing and expanding. The cities continue to grow upward and outward. Factories turn out the greatest abundance of goods in the world. The farms are the most productive on earth.

America—a beautiful land, a fertile land, a mighty land, a happy land.

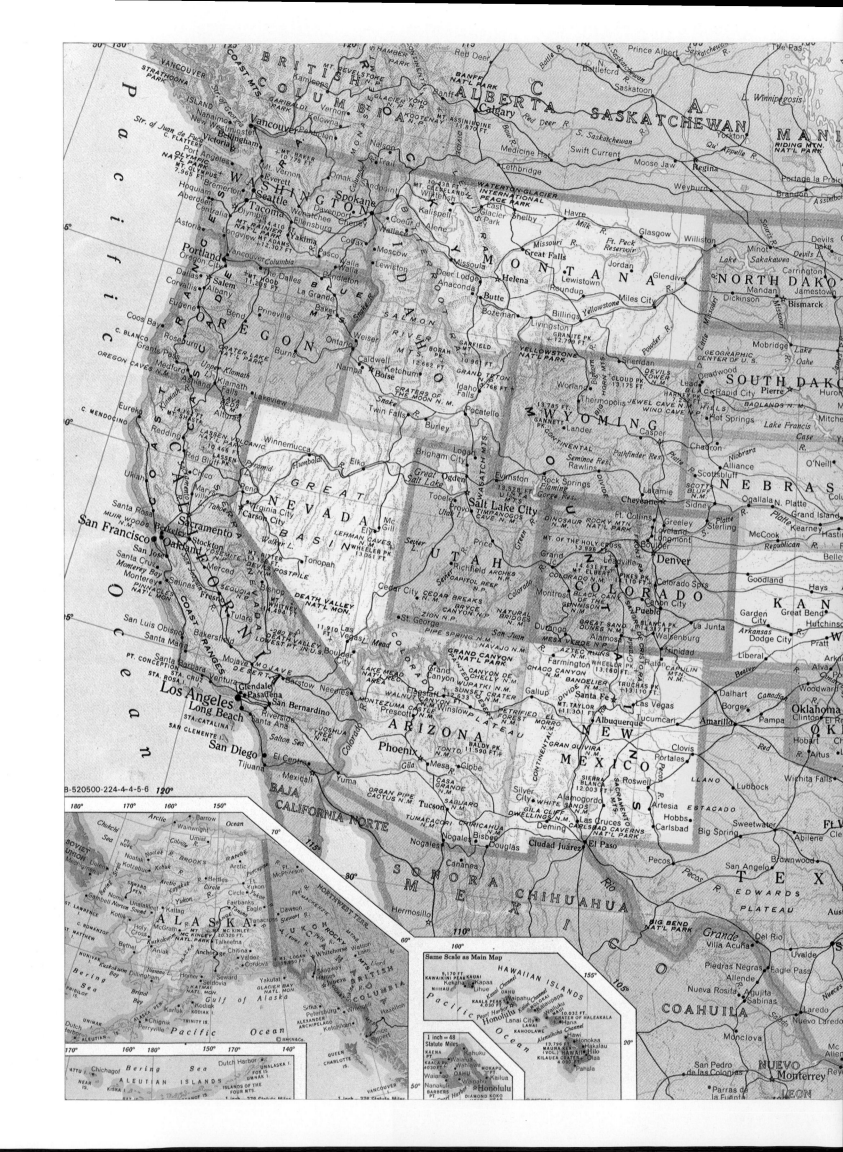

9

The leaves are beginning to change to their autumn color in Peacham, Vermont.

New England

Fishing boats at Rockport Harbor, Massachusetts. Rockport was settled in 1690 and has become, in addition to being a fishing village, an artists' colony. It is located at the tip of Cape Ann, north of Gloucester.

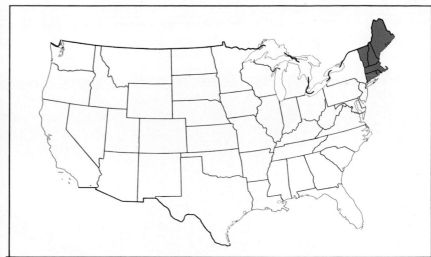

NEW ENGLAND

In the extreme northeast corner of the United States, six of the oldest states form the most homogeneous and clearly defined region in the whole country—Maine, New Hampshire, Vermont, Massachusetts, Rhode Island and Connecticut. Four were among the original 13 colonies and the other two were among the first new states in the Union.

Originally populated by Indians of the Algonquian Nation, this region of rugged mountains, watered by swift-flowing mountain streams and beautiful rivers, New England, was the place where the Pilgrim Fathers and their successors built their new homes. Despite the poor farming, the fishing was excellent and the forest rich in game and timber. The rivers supplied power for sawmills and for the factories which the practical and inventive 'Yankees' (a mysterious nickname given by the Dutch) were soon running.

New England today is highly industrialized and urbanized, yet it preserves much of its old early-American flavor. Its fishing fleet still brings in enormous catches of cod, mackerel and haddock. The picturesque fishing ports are favorite haunts of artists. Lovely old villages are still distinguished by the famous New England commons or greens and the New England churches —graceful and white, surmounted sometimes by a square bell tower, sometimes by a slender spire.

No region has more landmarks of America's struggle toward nationhood. Plymouth Rock marks the place where the Pilgrims landed after making the Mayflower Compact, America's first written instrument of democratic government. Successive waves of English colonists quickly made New England the most populous part of North America. Boston became the leading city of the New World and then the chief center of social resistance to the British Crown. Faneuil Hall, the Old North Church, the battlefields of Lexington and Concord, Bunker Hill and many more preserved sites and buildings commemorate the outbreak of the Revolution.

New England contains some of the country's most beautiful scenery—the wooded slopes of the Green Mountains of Vermont, the White Mountains of New Hampshire, the Berkshires of Massachusetts and Connecticut, the forest-covered primeval wilderness of Maine, the Connecticut River, flowing from Canada to Long Island Sound.

Pages 14-15: The autumn foliage turns in the front yard of a typical New England clapboard.

Opposite: New England is a land of mountains and foothills, all of which seem to explode in a blaze of reds, browns and yellows during October. Tourists make their 'autumn foliage tours' at this time and the old inns and taverns are packed. This is Montgomery Center, Vermont, population 681, about ten miles from the Canadian border.

Left: One of the historical buildings at Old Sturbridge Village in Massachusetts. Located near present-day Sturbridge, it is a recreation of a farming hamlet in Massachusetts in the early 1800s. Centered around the green are more than 40 old houses, shops and mills. Men and women in authentic Federal period dress explain the exhibits and work at crafts. The village is also a working farm, complete with crops and livestock.

Below: An early fall snow near Oxford, New Hampshire. Winter can come early in this part of New England, and it can be severe. In parts of the state the average January temperature is a mere 14 degrees, and the wind velocity at the top of Mount Washington has been clocked at 231 miles per hour, the highest on record in any state.

Overleaf: The outbuildings on a farm near East Hampton, Connecticut. The area of the Connecticut River Vally is fertile, with beautiful quiet lakes and hills.

The Middle Atlantic States

The skyline of Lower Manhattan at night.

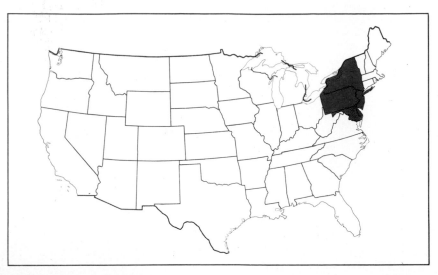

Below: Niagara Falls on the American side. In the distance is Niagara Falls, Ontario. The falls are the most-visited, most-honeymooned attractions on the North American Continent. The American Falls are 193 feet high and 1000 feet wide, and are separated from the Canadian Falls by Goat Island. From this island an elevator descends to the Cave of the Winds, where visitors put on raincoats and boots to go on a special walkway in front of the American Falls. The view is spectacular.

Opposite: The Statue of Liberty in New York Harbor; in the distance are the twin towers of the World Trade Center. The statue was given to the United States by the French people. Designed by Frederic Bartholdi, it is 152 feet high and its base on Liberty Island is about the same height. The statue itself is made of copper and the framework was designed by Gustav Eiffel, the designer of the Eiffel Tower in Paris.

THE MIDDLE ATLANTIC STATES

Along the Atlantic Coast between New England and the South lie five states—New York, New Jersey, Pennsylvania, Maryland, Delaware, plus the District of Columbia—whose total area represents only about one-thirtieth of the American land surface, but which contains nearly a fifth of the population. This busy, populous seaboard region includes the nation's largest city, New York City; its fourth largest city, Philadelphia; and five other cities with a metro area population of over one million—Washington DC, Pittsburgh, Baltimore, Newark and Buffalo.

Though the Eastern Coastal Plain is a virtually solid metropolitan belt of industrial centers and suburbs, the five states also have handsome countryside—mountains, woods, lakes and valleys. The Catskills, Poconos, Adirondacks and other Appalachian ranges offer some of the finest resort areas in the world. Side by side with the urban centers stretch miles of the world's richest farmland.

It is a region rich in history. All the states were among the original thirteen. Washington and his army spent nearly the entire Revolutionary War in this area. Philadelphia's Independence Square preserves the memories of the Declaration of Independence and the Constitutional Convention. But the most extensive historical site in the region dates from another crisis in America's history—the Civil War. The Battlefield at Gettysburg, Pennsylvania is preserved as a national military park.

Opposite: The Washington Monument dominates the Mall in Washington DC and seems to tower over the Capitol Dome on the horizon. This obelisk is precisely 555 feet, 5 1/8 inches high, and is said to be the tallest masonry structure in the world.

Left: The Lincoln Memorial in Washington is built like a Greek temple and faces the Washington Monument across a long reflecting pool. The 19-foot statue of Lincoln by Daniel Chester French looks as though it had been carved from a single block of marble; it is actually 28 separate pieces. The Memorial was opened in 1922.

Below: Cherry blossoms in front of the Jefferson Memorial at the Tidal Basin in Washington.

Right: A Pennsylvania farm in the Pocono Mountains. This area of old, relatively low mountains not only is fine farming country, but it is a resort area, with year-round activities, drawing swimmers, fishermen and skiers from all over the East Coast.

Opposite: Independence Hall in Philadelphia. It is a part of Independence National Historical Park, a group of Colonial buildings centered around Independence Square at Sixth and Chestnut Streets. Actually, Independence Hall is the old State House, and it was here where the Declaration of Independence and the United States Constitution were signed, and where George Washington accepted command of the Continental Armies. The capital of the United States from 1796 to 1800, Philadelphia was once the second largest city in the English-speaking world. The city was founded by William Penn in 1682 as a Quaker colony. He named his 'Greene Countrie Towne' Philadelphia, a Greek name that means 'City of Brotherly Love.'

Below: A covered bridge in Pennsylvania. There are many theories about why covered bridges were built. One theory states that they were covered to keep the sun and the rain from the bridge bed in order to slow down the rotting of the timbers. Another says that in colder regions the snow would build up faster on bridges than on the roads because of the melting effect of the dirt under the road. In any event, in winter, snow had to be shoveled onto the bridge so the sleighs could pass.

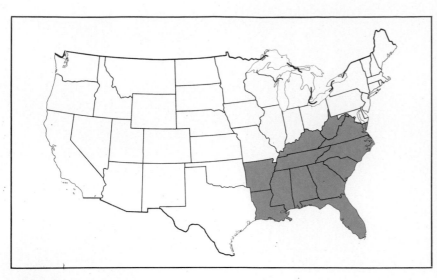

THE SOUTH

The 12 Southern States—Georgia, North Carolina, South Carolina, Kentucky, Virginia, West Virginia, Florida, Alabama, Mississippi, Louisiana, Arkansas and Tennessee—are rich in history and beauty. From the first permanent English settlement in America, founded at Jamestown in 1607, slowly grew a large and prosperous colony named Virginia, stretching west to the Mississippi River. Ultimately it was carved into three states—Virginia, West Virginia and Kentucky.

The first explorers of this vast region were Spanish. Ponce de León's exploration of both Florida coasts was followed by Hernando de Soto's 4000-mile trek into the interior, in which he penetrated the future states of Georgia, Tennessee, Alabama and Mississippi before discovering and crossing the Mississippi. In 1565 the first permanent settlement of the future United States by Europeans was accomplished by the Spaniards at St Augustine, Florida. Farther west a French settlement took root at New Orleans early in the eighteenth century. Early English settlements at Charleston, Savannah, Wilmington and elsewhere also survive.

Although the South was the earliest part of the United States to be settled by Europeans, it is only within the last few decades that its rich history, its balmy climate, its food, entertainment and hospitality have made it an important tourist area. The 12 states run the gamut from mile-high forested mountain peaks to rolling farmlands to palm-shaded subtropical beaches.

The South is the only region in the United States equally rich in historic souvenirs from the two great crisis of American history—the Revolution and the Civil War.

Right: A mill on Glade Creek in West Virginia, the state that has been described as 'the most southern of the northern, the most northern of the southern, the most western of the eastern, the most eastern of the western states.'

Previous Spread: The Orton Plantation House in North Carolina. The plantation manor house, with its tall pillars and portico in front, is an architectural reminder of the South of the past.

Left: The 215-foot high stone bridge near Natural Bridge, Virginia. Before the settlers came, Indians worshipped this phenomenon of nature. Thomas Jefferson bought the gorge and the bridge for 20 shillings in 1774, building a cabin for visitors and hiring caretakers to maintain the tourist attraction.

Opposite: A scene in the Blue Ridge Mountains of Virginia, overlooking the Shenandoah Valley.

Below: 'Monticello,' the mansion that Thomas Jefferson designed for himself, is one of the most beautiful estates in Virginia and is considered a classic of American architecture. Begun in 1769, it took 40 years for Jefferson to complete. It was here that he took his bride, Martha, in 1772, and it was here that he died on 4 July 1826. The house contains many of his inventions, such as dumb-waiters, hidden stairways and a clock operated by cannonball weights.

Previous spread: A thoroughbred racehorse farm in the Bluegrass Region of Kentucky.

Left: Canoers in the Okefenokee Swamp in southeast Georgia, near Waycross. The Okefenokee is the largest preserved fresh-water swampland in the United States, covering 700 square miles. The early Creek Indians called it 'The Land of the Trembling Earth,' and its lakes of dark brown water, lush with moss-draped cypress trees and mysterious streams are the headwaters of the Suwannee River, about which Stephen Collins Foster waxed so eloquently.

Opposite: Miami Beach, Florida, sometimes called 'America's International Playground,' where celebrities and sunbathers are squeezed onto an island a mere eight miles long and from one to three miles wide. This is Hotel Row, where property sells for thousands of dollars per front foot. It is hard to believe that it was once a palmetto swamp, populated mostly by snakes and mosquitoes, until John S Collins failed in his attempt to grow avocados there and turned to real estate. He auctioned off the land (much of it underwater), brought sand to turn it into solid ground, and built what was then the longest wooden bridge in the United States, to connect it with Miami.

Below: The Everglades, stretching over 2100 square miles, in southern Florida, is the largest subtropical wilderness in North America. It is a spectacular area—half land, half water. Indians called it 'River of Grass.'

Left: Decatur Street in New Orleans' French Quarter, the *Vieux Carré*, or 'Old Square.'

Below: Apartment houses in the French Quarter of New Orleans show their typically intricate wrought-iron work. In this section of New Orleans every house and shop has its own special history. Many *Vieux Carré* homes turn their backs on the streets and open out into flagstoned patios shaded by palms and banana plants. In this private world, the family has breakfast, the housewife does her chores, and cool drinks are served on a summer's evening. The population is cosmopolitan with its Creoles (descendants of the original French and Spanish colonists), Cajuns (descendants of the Acadians who were driven from Nova Scotia by the British in 1755) and other groups whose ancestors came from the Caribbean and Africa.

The Midwest and
the Plains

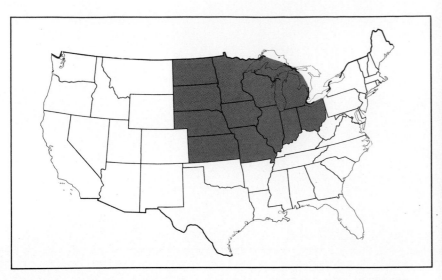

THE MIDWEST AND THE PLAINS

There are eight Midwest States—Ohio, Indiana, Illinois, Michigan, Wisconsin, Minnesota, Iowa and Missouri—and four Plains States—North Dakota, South Dakota, Nebraska and Kansas. Combined, the two sections make up a huge part of the continent and have a population of some 62 million.

The region is broad and flat, with many clusters of rolling hills. The northern stretch is studded with lakes and surviving patches of the magnificent forest the first explorers found. Early French explorers and trappers dotted the area with French names—Eau Claire, Terre Haute, Pierre, Detroit, Fond du Lac, St Louis and Vincennes, Indiana, which was the scene of George Rogers Clark's Revolutionary War victory which helped insure that part of the vast region would be a part of the new United States. The end of that war was a signal for tremendous immigration from the Eastern Seaboard. Ohio became a state in 1803, the same year that the Louisiana Purchase gave the vast trans-Mississippi area to the Union.

The first European visitors west of the Mississippi were Coronado and his men in 1541, but it was not until the journey of Marquette and Joliet in 1634 that the real penetration began. During the late seventeenth and early eighteenth centuries, French fur traders roamed Kansas and Nebraska and by 1743 entered the Dakotas, and in 1804 Lewis and Clark made their historical exploration of the Louisiana Purchase—that gigantic real estate bargain. Settlers followed and by the 1840s Kansas was a jumping-off point for covered wagon trains headed west.

Almost everything can be found in the region, except salt water. Huge cities and small towns, major coal, oil and gas deposits, iron ore ranges, diversified factories, magnificent wheat and corn fields, acres of oats, rye, flaxseed, soybeans, sugar beets, fruit, livestock and dairies.

Previous spread: A farm in the south central part of Wisconsin. Much of the area contains rolling hills that are the result of glacial moraines—extremely fertile formations.

Right: A Kansas wheat field. In 1981 Kansas produced 305 million bushels of this crop, second only to North Dakota. Kansas's total was almost 12 percent of all the wheat grown in the United States that year.

Left: Downtown Chicago at night. This huge city on the shores of Lake Michigan is the chief metropolis of the center of the country. The lakeshore is the city's showcase, with a superb chain of parks and parkways flanking the shore, and the city's tallest and finest buildings rising behind them. Chicago was the birthplace of the modern skyscraper and contains many notable examples of modern architecture and engineering, including the imposing Standard Oil Building in the center, which rises to a height of 1454 feet, making it the tallest building in the world. To the right of it, with the two poles on top, is the John Hancock Center—1127 feet tall.

Below: One of the most beautiful landmarks in Chicago is Buckingham Fountain in Grant Park. Also in the park, which is located between Lake Michigan and the heart of the city, are the John G Shedd Aquarium, the Adler Planetarium and the distinguished Art Institute of Chicago.

Left: Mount Rushmore National Memorial. The faces of Washington, Jefferson, Theodore Roosevelt and Lincoln were carved in the granite mountain by Gutzon Borglum. Each head is 60 feet from chin to forehead.

Opposite top: The exotic rock formations in the Dells of the Wisconsin River.

Opposite bottom: The shores of Lake Superior in Minnesota. Superior, like all the Great Lakes, is a freshwater sea. But with its 31,700 square mile area, it is second in size only to the Caspian Sea.

Below: A view of the frozen Manitou River near Lake Superior in Minnesota.

Above: The Straits of Mackinac join Lake Huron and Lake Michigan. Soaring over the wide channel is the third longest suspension bridge in North America—the Mackinac Bridge. This point is the only place in America where the sun rises on one Great Lake (Huron) and sets on another (Michigan). Mackinaw City began as a French trading post and became Fort Michilimackinac about 1715. It was taken over by the British in 1761 and two years later was captured by Indians. St Ignace was founded over three hundred years ago by the French priest-explorer, Father Marquette. It is also the gateway to Michigan's splendidly beautiful Upper Peninsula with its striking scenery.

Opposite: Holland, Michigan has the largest concentration of people of Dutch descent in America. Each May, its Tulip Festival draws thousands of visitors to see thousands of acres of blooming tulips and to watch Dutch ceremonies, which include street scrubbing, clog dancing and parades in native costumes.

Left: A view of Mackinac Island, Michigan, in the Straits of Mackinac, the most famous of the hundreds of islands in Michigan, sometimes called 'The Bermuda of the North.' Held by the French until 1760, it became English after Wolfe's victory at Québec, was turned over to the US at the end of the Revolution, was British during the War of 1812, and then reverted.

Right: Indiana has its covered bridges, too. This one is now used merely for walking. It dates back to 1876 and is located in Parke County, near Rockville.

Opposite: Looking across the Mississippi River toward St Louis, the most striking thing that one sees is the mammoth Gateway Arch, symbolizing the city's nickname of 'The Gateway to the West.' An architectural marvel that soars to 630 feet, the stainless steel arch has an observation deck on the top which features a spectacular view.

Below: A winter scene on a farm in Porter County, Indiana, near Valparaiso.

Sunset near New River, Arizona. The giant Saguaro cactus in the foreground produces a bloom that is Arizona's state flower.

The Southwest and Southern California

One of the arches in Arches National Park near Moab, Utah. In the background are the snow-capped peaks of the La Sal Mountains.

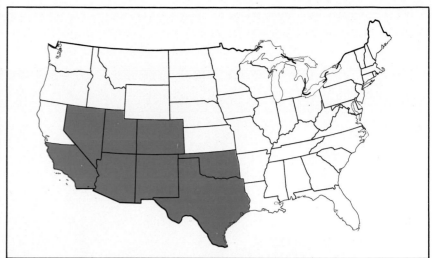

THE SOUTHWEST AND SOUTHERN CALIFORNIA

The Southwest contains seven states—Oklahoma, Texas, New Mexico, Arizona, Nevada, Utah and Colorado, plus Southern California. Most of the Southwest was once consigned to the Indians as worthless, but today it is a rich, varied and interesting region, growing more rapidly than that of any other part of the country.

This is not to say that the wide open spaces are disappearing. The magnificent vistas in which formations 50 miles away seem near at hand are still there. Bald, 12,000-foot-high mountains fringed with thick ponderosa pine and aspen forests rise within sight of the awe-inspiring, mile-deep Grand Canyon. Jagged, twisted lava beds spewed out by now-extinct volcanoes scar terrain that edges flowering meadows. Mesquite groves crowd spiny cacti while palm leaves fan back-yard patios. Earth-moving rivers like the Colorado and the Rio Grande—plus scores of sky-blue, man-made lakes and a few natural ones—water some of the most arid landscape in North America. Sand dunes, waterfalls, hot springs, geysers, salt flats, earthquake faults, glaciers and natural bridges are among the wonders of this region, whose lowest point is in Death Valley (282 feet below sea level) and whose highest point is more than 14,000 feet at Mount Whitney in California and Mount Elbert in Colorado.

Aside from an occasional fur trapper or explorer, the northern part of this region belonged to the Indians until well into the nineteenth century. Two major elements contributed to the wave of colonization near the middle of that century: the Mormon emigration and a succession of gold and silver strikes.

The southern part of this region was explored earlier. In 1540, a year after Friar Marcos de Niza had made a preliminary exploration into Arizona and New Mexico, Coronado led an expedition in search of the fabled Seven Cities of Cibola. Coronado did not find them, of course, but he laid the foundation for Spanish rule over the region for nearly three centuries.

Today, where Spanish conquistadores once vainly searched for gold and where French-Canadian trappers took pelts, fabulous bonanzas of oil and gas flow from the ground. Where hard-riding cowboys once herded cattle on the Long Drive, space scientists work on the frontier of technology.

Left: The Alamo is in downtown San Antonio. It was the site of the battle between Santa Anna and the Texans—1836.

Below left: The serpentine San Antonio River flows through the heart of the city. This is the River Walk.

This picture: The moon over downtown Dallas.

Above: Moonrise over Santa Fe, New Mexico. Founded by Spaniards about 1610 on an old Indian pueblo, Santa Fe, the capital of New Mexico, is said to be the oldest seat of government in America. It is situated on a high rolling tableland dotted with piñon pines and backed by the lofty Sangre de Cristo Mountains.

Left: The Rio Chama flows through a mountain valley in northern New Mexico to join the Rio Grande.

Below: Adobe buildings at Taos Pueblo, New Mexico. These multi-storied communal dwellings are located on a high plateau flanked by the Sangre de Cristo Mountains which rise to 13,161 feet at nearby Wheeler Peak, the highest elevation in the State of New Mexico. Also nearby are the ruins of the Mission of San Geronimo de Taos, founded in 1610.

Massive sand dunes outside hot, dry Yuma, Arizona. Movie companies have often used this desert for location shots.

Left: The dramatic Canyon de Chelly in Arizona is now a national monument. This impressive preserve, where sheer, red sandstone walls rise as high as a thousand feet above the canyon floor and gigantic formations stand taller than an 80-story building, shows Indian civilization from the early Anasazi Period, about 350 AD, through thirteenth-century cliff dwellings. When William of Normandy defeated the English at the Battle of Hastings in 1066, Pueblo Indians had already built dwellings in these walls.

Opposite: Monument Valley covers several thousand square miles on both sides of the Utah-Arizona state line. It has become famous for its giant red sandstone monoliths and spires rising several thousand feet above the surrounding plains of the Navajo Reservation. This colorful valley with the sandstone pillars and spires that resemble huge temple ruins has often been the site of moving picture location camps. Director John Ford used it many times for the background for his western films, often starring John Wayne.

Below: Red Rock Crossing near Sedona, Arizona. Located in Oak Creek Canyon, which begins south of Flagstaff and continues for a dozen miles to Sedona, the canyon opens up into a gorgeous, rock-rimmed amphitheater that has also been used as a background for many Western movies. The stream is spectacular, especially for fishermen.

Preceding spread: Rocky Mountain National Park, near Estes, Colorado, sits astride the Continental Divide. It is a land of snow-capped mountain ranges, sparkling lakes, pine and fir and quaking aspen, elk, deer and bighorn sheep. Trail Ridge Road, a wide and beautiful highway, crosses the park and drops down the west side of the Divide to Grand Lake. Among many other sights, the Mummy Range, the Never Summer Range, Iceberg Lake and Specimen Mountain are seen from the Trail Ridge Road.

Above: The towering 12,000-foot-high San Francisco Peaks can be seen from Coconino National Forest near Flagstaff, Arizona. The forest surrounds the city of Flagstaff, and Arizona's highest point, Humphreys Peak, is here, as is Lake of Cinders, a 640,000 square-foot moonscape that was created by the United States Geological Survey. Other outstanding scenic areas include parts of the Mogollon Rim and the Verde River Valley, part of the Sycamore Canyon Wilderness area, extinct volcanoes and lava beds. This is where Zane Grey wrote his novel, *Call of the Canyon.*

Opposite: In this tight, peak-rimmed valley near Silverton, Colorado, one can see the Needle Mountains in the Rocky Mountain Chain.

Right: The Twin Falls in the Yankee Bay Basin in the Colorado Rockies near Ouray lie in a natural basin surrounded by the 12,000 to 13,000-foot peaks of the San Juan Mountains of the Rocky Mountain Chain.

Above: Downtown Las Vegas, Nevada, in the early morning. The largest city in the state, it spreads over a desert plain east of the Charleston Range. Big, brassy, and aglow with neon lighting, Las Vegas is a round-the-clock, year-round resort. Its bars and casinos—with roulette wheels, slot machines, crap and poker games, faro, chuckaluck and other games of chance—operate 24 hours a day. Luxurious hotels on the 'Strip' stage elaborate shows for their customers.

Left: The living is easy—and expensive—in Palm Springs, California.

Below: The highest dam in the world—Hoover Dam, near Las Vegas.

Above: Mission Bay Park at San Diego, California, which houses Sea World, one of the country's finest marine parks. The chief attractions are The Theater of the Sea, Sea Grotto and Lagoon. San Diego has been called 'the place where California began' because the Portuguese conquistador Cabrillo landed here in 1542. The southernmost city in California has a Mexican flavor because of its proximity to Mexico's border town of Tijuana. San Diego stretches from the Pacific Ocean eastward over lovely rolling hills; its balmy climate encourages outdoor living.

Right: A helicopter view of the vast orange groves in Riverside County, California. The orange industry here dates back to 1873, when a resident of the new town of Riverside got two cuttings of a new type of orange, a mutation that had been developed in Brazil.

Opposite: The Junipero Serra Museum in San Diego, which houses a collection that traces the history of the California missions. The museum was named for Junipero Serra, the Franciscan who founded the first of these missions in San Diego in 1769, and is located in Presidio Park. The museum also serves as a place to begin a tour of the San Diego Missions, the most famous of which are the Mission Basilica San Diego de Alcala, the Mission San Antonio de Pala, the Mission San Luis Rey de Francia and the Old Mission San Juan Capistrano.

Left: The coastline at Los Angeles. Land is so expensive here that individual house lots are quite small, and waterfront property is at a premium.

Opposite: A scenic view of suburban homes at the Hollywood Reservoir in Los Angeles. The city began as a sleepy Spanish village. On 4 September 1781, Don Felipe de Neve, Governor of California, marched to the site of the present city and with solemn ceremonies founded 'The Town of Our Lady the Queen of the Angels of Porciuncula' — now shortened to 'Los Angeles.' The city grew to its present enormous size in relatively recent years, partly by absorbing neighboring communities. One of these was Hollywood, legendary center of the film industry and modern television production. In the half-century between 1890 and 1940, the city grew from 50,395 to 1,504,277 — a gain of 2,645.7 percent. It now has almost three million residents.

Below: Los Angeles at night. Los Angeles is the largest city in the United States in area and second largest in population in its metropolitan area. Spreading for miles inland and along the ocean, this great city is the center of far-flung orange groves and of an important oil-producing area. It is rich in manufactures, with a fine harbor, and its superb beaches are an unexcelled resort attraction. Besides all this, it is the world's capital of the movie industry.

The Northwest and Northern California

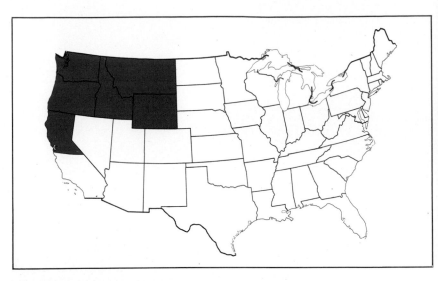

THE NORTHWEST AND NORTHERN CALIFORNIA

There are five states — Oregon, Washington, Idaho, Montana and Wyoming — in the Northwest, plus Northern California. Few regions in the world can match this area for variety and number of natural wonders — a rain forest wilderness, groves of giant trees, glaciers, raging rivers flowing through deep gorges, great craggy mountain peaks, active volcanoes, scorching deserts.

It is one of the most productive regions of the world. In Northern California, Washington and Oregon are orchards, cattle ranges, limitless wheat fields. In Idaho, Montana and Wyoming are vast ranches and underground riches.

Exotic place names give clues to the region's historical background. In Northern California most of the major cities have Spanish names — San Francisco, Sacramento, San José. In other states there are reminders of the French fur trappers — Grand Coulee, Coeur d'Alene.

Dwellings and other structures tell the story of the land's settlement. The Spanish contributed the thick-walled, comfortable adobe houses. A New Englander in Monterey added galleries to a typical Yankee home and created the Monterey style. Russians descending the coast from Alaska built forts and churches. Chinese mine workers built joss houses and temples, French and Italian wine makers added stone wineries. Lumber barons and rich ranchers dotted the landscape with great Victorian mansions, while lumberjacks hewed out log cabins.

Previous spread: Horses graze in Grand Teton National Park, Wyoming. Its 485 square-miles include some of the most breathtaking landscape in North America. Within the park are the alpine-like, glacier-carved Grand Teton Mountains, with their jagged peaks and intervening canyons; a dozen glaciers; eight large lakes; extensive fir, spruce and pine forests and summits ranging from 11,000 to nearly 14,000 feet above sea level.

Right: Yellowstone Falls in Yellowstone National Park, Wyoming — the oldest and most noted of the federal preserves.

The Great Fountain Geyser beginning to erupt —
Yellowstone National Park.

Right: A view in Glacier National Park, Montana, which has gorgeous scenery, clear mountain lakes, and active glaciers. Located on Montana's Canadian border, this 1600 square-mile park is a glacier-carved Rocky Mountain wonderland. The park has 60 small glaciers in the process of disappearing, and nearly 200 glacier-formed lakes. Alpine flowers can be found there, as well as white mountain goat, elk, moose, bighorn sheep, deer and bear. The park is part of the Waterton-Glacier International Peace Park, established by the United States and Canada in 1932.

Opposite: Rising Sun Mountain in Glacier National Park.

Below: The Many Glacier Hotel at Grinnel Point in Glacier National Park, overlooking Swiftcurrent Lake. Big, rugged and primitive, Glacier National Park is nature's unspoiled domain. Man and his civilization are reduced to insignificance by the wild grandeur of these million acres. Declared a national park on 11 May 1910, the park, with its spectacular scenery, is preserved year after year much as it was when Meriwether Lewis saw it in the distance in 1806. Therefore, it is easy to get lost, once off the trail, and some of the wild animals can be dangerous. This is a land where winter does not beat a full retreat until mid-June, and sometimes returns in mid-September. Snowbanks line the road in July.

Left: The lone cypress along the 17-mile drive on the Monterey Peninsula near Carmel, California. The Drive is a scenic one and stretches between Monterey and Carmel along the Pacific Coast.

Opposite: A California winery in the Napa Valley, north of San Francisco. Most California vineyards conduct tours of the premises, followed by wine tasting sessions.

Below: The Golden Gate Bridge, with San Francisco in the distance. Built in 1937, the bridge is second only to the Verrazano-Narrows bridge in New York City in length for a suspension bridge. It connects San Francisco with the mainland to the north.

Above: A winter view of the Half Dome in Yosemite Valley, California. This valley, in Yosemite National Park with its 757,000 acres of beauty, is the one that many call the world's most beautiful valley. The park, in California's High Sierras, contains mountains, canyons, lakes, waterfalls and icy streams. The valley, walled by towering granite cliffs and monoliths such as Half Dome and El Capitan, is accentuated by the Mariposa grove of gaint sequoia trees. It is the home of mule deer and black bear.

Right: Yosemite in winter.

Below: Yosemite Falls has a height of 2,425 feet, but it is really three waterfalls, having two leaps. It is a cascade type of waterfall, therefore, and it does reduce to a trickle or become dry for part of each year. Nevertheless, it is the third highest waterfall in the world. John Muir, the founder of the park, wrote that here are 'the most songful streams of the world.'

Left: All along the northern half of California's coast, the redwood forests are spectacular. From Mill Creek Redwoods State Park in the North to the Big Basin Redwoods State Park south of San Francisco, the coastal area is a series of state parks and groves. These shown are found near Crescent City, California, in Redwood National Park. The park stretches for 46 miles and is about seven miles in width. It includes 30 miles of coastline. There are also three state parks near Crescent City that contain redwoods. They are the Jedediah Smith Redwoods State Park, the Del Norte Coast Redwoods State Park and Prairie Creek Redwoods State Park.

Opposite: A grove of giant sequoia trees in Yosemite National Park, California.

Below: Crater Lake in the Oregon Cascades. Crater Lake National Park is one of the scenic wonders of America. The waters of the lake, 1996 feet deep, are crystal clear and intensely blue. Hemmed in by steep mountain walls and towering forests, the lake lies 6000 feet above sea level in a sunken volcanic crater. The park is Oregon's most notable visitor attraction. It is in the heart of the Cascade Range, 55 miles northwest of Klamath Falls. Its 250 square-miles are superbly wooded, and contain peaks rising to more than 8000 feet that guard the unique and incredibly blue jewel that is Crater Lake.

Right: Mount Ranier, south of Seattle, Washington, rises from near sea level to 14,410 feet. It is a dormant volcano, and is the dominant natural feature of the State of Washington. It is located in Mount Rainier National Park, which also has permanent snow fields, high meadows, crystal clear lakes and a great variety of trees and flowers. The park is located in the Cascade Range of mountains.

Opposite: A scenic view in Olympic National Park, Washington. This occupies the heart of the Olympic Peninsula on the northwest coast of the state between the Pacific Ocean and Puget Sound. It is a vast area, having zones ranging from temperate rain forests to mountain glaciers, and it preserves native plant and animal life.

Below: Downtown Seattle, Washington, is dominated by the Space Needle (right). The needle, with its high observation deck, is located in Seattle Center, which was built for the 1962 Seattle World's Fair. Seattle is the metropolis of Washington and the Pacific Northwest. Its salt-water harbor of Elliott Bay is rimmed by port facilities for the largest ocean-going vessels. It has a fresh-water harbor for fishing and pleasure boats. Scenic boulevards link waterfronts with hilltops and provide views of distant mountains. Its industries are varied — lumbering, airplane manufacturing, aluminum fabrication, shipbuilding and others.

Mt McKinley, the highest mountain in North
America at 20,320 feet, and Mt Hunter, at 14,573
feet, tower over the Kahiltna Glacier in Alaska.

Alaska and Hawaii

ALASKA AN[D]

America's two newest [states] [...] and Hawaii (admitted in [...] not contiguous with the [...]

Alaska is huge, its 58[...] the size of the next lar[gest...] residents, with only a l[...]

Alaska's position on t[...] portion of the North [...] farther west than Ho[...] western of the Alaskan [...] New Zealand. In latit[...] distance north as Stoc[...] northernmost point of t[...] Cape in Norway.

Alaska was discovere[d...] navigator under contra[ct...] 1867, the United Stat[es...] offered Russia $7.2 mil[...] the American flag was [...]

Hawaii is the only sta[te...] exception of South Flor[...] climate. Discovered by [...] originally called the San[...] in 1898 and made it a t[...]

Left: Kauai Island has the largest rivers of any of the Hawaiian Islands. One of them, the Wailua, on the east coast, provides scenic sightseeing journeys through a lush tropical setting, including strange fern grottoes and this magnificent waterfall.

Opposite: The Island of Maui is often called the 'Valley Island' because many canyons cut into the two volcanic mountains that form the island. There are also smaller mountains on the island, such as this one, Iao Needle. Between the mountains is a broad, low isthmus with sugar cane and pineapple plantations. The highest point on Maui is 10,023-foot Haleakala, the center of the Haleakala National Forest.

Above: Waikiki Beach in Honolulu. The beach extends along the seashore of the Harbor of Honolulu to the famous Diamond Head Crater in the distance. Surfboard riding, swimming and sailing are favorites here, and the hotels and beach of Waikiki, an eastern suburb of Honolulu, constitute the best-known tourist resort. Honolulu is the most southern and farthest west city in the United States, after Nome, and has been the island capital for more than 100 years. It is situated on the Island of Oahu. Out of the approximately 965,000 people in the whole state, some 38 percent of them live in the city of Honolulu.

Overleaf: Sunset on Anaehoomalu Bay, Hawaii.